THE BIG GAME

NBA AND WNBA
FINALS

— BASKETBALL'S BIGGEST PLAYOFFS —

Matt Scheff

Lerner Publications ◆ Minneapolis

Lerner Publications Company
An imprint of Lerner Publishing Group, Inc.
241 First Avenue North
Minneapolis, MN 55401 USA

For reading levels and more information, look up this title at www.lernerbooks.com.

Main body text set in Conduit ITC Std.
Typeface provided by International Typeface Corp.

Editor: Alison Lorenz **Designer:** Viet Chu

Library of Congress Cataloging-in-Publication Data

Names: Scheff, Matt, author.
Title: NBA and WNBA Finals: Basketball's Biggest Playoffs / Matt Scheff.
Description: Minneapolis : Lerner Publications, 2021. | Series: The big game (Lerner sports) | Includes bibliographical references and index. | Audience: Ages 7–11 | Audience: Grades 4–6 | Summary: "Follow the spectacular shots, thrilling comebacks, and monumental moments of basketball's most exciting games. Readers learn about the biggest NBA and WNBA finals, the leagues' history, and the amazing feats of the sport's best stars"— Provided by publisher.
Identifiers: LCCN 2019030053 | ISBN 9781541597594 (library binding) | ISBN 9781728401232 (ebook)
Subjects: LCSH: Basketball—United States—History—Juvenile literature. | National Basketball Association—Juvenile literature. |
Basketball—Tournaments—United States—History—Juvenile literature.
Classification: LCC GV885.1 .S334 2020 | DDC 796.323—dc23

LC record available at https://lccn.loc.gov/2019030053

Manufactured in the United States of America
1-47863-48303-12/13/2019

Contents

The Raptors' Kawhi Leonard goes for a dunk at the 2019 Finals.

A New Era

The action was frantic in Game 4 of the 2019 National Basketball Association (NBA) Finals. The Toronto Raptors held a 2–1 lead in the series. The Golden State Warriors clung to a four-point lead.

Early in the second half, Toronto got a rebound and pushed the ball up the court. Fred VanVleet zipped a pass to Kawhi Leonard. Leonard rose up and took a three-point shot. *Swish!* Seconds later, Leonard stole the ball from a Golden State player. He dribbled up the court and fired another shot with a defender in his face. It was good! Leonard's quick six points gave his team the lead. The Warriors never recovered, and the Raptors were on their way to their first NBA title.

- The NBA formed in 1949, and the Women's National Basketball Association (WNBA) formed in 1996.

- The Boston Celtics have the most championship titles of any team in the NBA. In the WNBA, the Houston Comets and the Minnesota Lynx have the most titles.

- Michael Jordan and Cynthia Cooper are the ultimate Finals most valuable players (MVPs). Jordan won the Finals MVP award a record six times. Cooper won it a record four times.

- Fans tune in to the NBA Finals in more than 200 countries and 50 languages. In 2017, nearly one million people watched the WNBA Finals.

The Boston Celtics' Bill Russell dunks the ball against the Philadelphia 76ers in 1965.

CHAPTER 1

THE FINALS

IN 1949, THE BASKETBALL ASSOCIATION OF AMERICA (BAA) merged with the National Basketball League to form the NBA. Every year since, two teams have faced off in the NBA Finals. Center George Mikan and the Minneapolis Lakers dominated in the early 1950s. The Lakers moved to Los Angeles before the 1960–1961 season. From 1957 to 1969, center Bill Russell led the Boston Celtics to 11 NBA championships, including eight in a row!

In the 1980s, Magic Johnson and the Lakers battled Larry Bird and the Celtics. Michael Jordan thrilled fans as he carried the Chicago Bulls to six titles in the 1990s. And in the 2010s, Stephen Curry helped make the Golden State Warriors the team to beat.

Michael Jordan's scoring average of more than 30 points per game is the highest ever in the NBA.

Inside the Game

Since the first BAA Finals in 1947, the Lakers and Celtics have ruled the league. The Celtics have won a record 17 titles, while the Lakers have 16. The two teams have won almost half of all the NBA titles.

The WNBA

The WNBA formed in 1996. Like the NBA, the WNBA has been a league of dynasties built around star players. Cynthia Cooper led the Houston Comets to the league's first four championship titles. In the first decade of the 2000s, the Los Angeles Sparks, Detroit Shock, and Phoenix Mercury racked up wins. And in the 2010s, Maya Moore powered the Minnesota Lynx to the top of the WNBA.

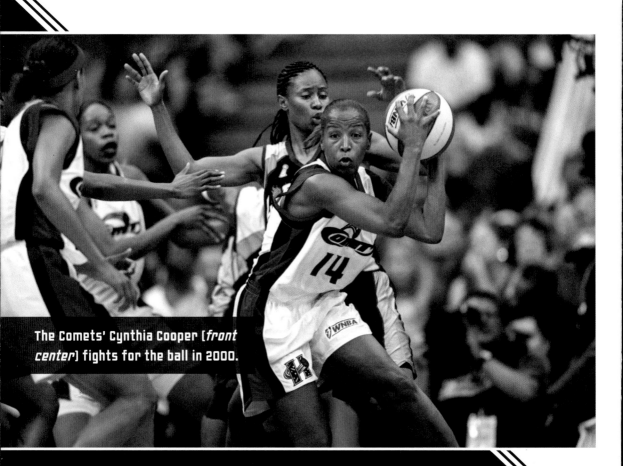

The Comets' Cynthia Cooper (*front center*) fights for the ball in 2000.

Maya Moore of the Minnesota Lynx

CHAPTER 2

The Greatest Moments

THE NBA AND WNBA FINALS DELIVER THRILLING AND memorable moments. One of the best came in 1970. The New York Knicks and Los Angeles Lakers were tied at three games. New York's chances looked dim for the winner-take-all Game 7. In Game 5, star forward Willis Reed had torn a muscle in his leg. Without Reed, the Knicks couldn't stop Lakers center Wilt Chamberlain.

But Reed surprised everyone by limping onto the court for Game 7. Though slowed by his injury, he scored the game's first basket. His defense was enough to slow down Chamberlain. Thanks to Reed, the Knicks won 113–99 and claimed their first NBA title.

Game 3 of the 2015 WNBA Finals was a nail-biter. The crowd was on its feet as the Indiana Fever took on the Minnesota Lynx. The game featured 11 ties and eight lead changes. In the final minute, Indiana had the ball with the game tied 77–77. Shenise Johnson launched a three-point shot. But it rattled off the rim. Minnesota took the ball.

Moore takes a shot in Game 3 of the 2015 WNBA Finals.

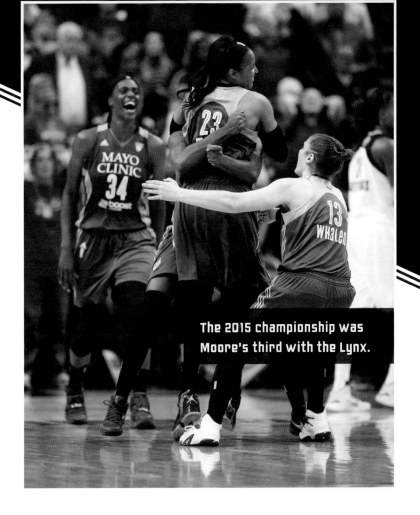

The 2015 championship was Moore's third with the Lynx.

Just 1.7 seconds remained. Minnesota guard Lindsay Whalen threw a pass to Maya Moore. Moore faked a shot, fooling her defender. She took one dribble to her right and shot the ball. The three-pointer sailed through the rim as time expired. The other Lynx swarmed Moore to celebrate. Two games later, the Lynx finished the job and won the series.

The Flu Game

The Chicago Bulls and Utah Jazz were tied at two games in the 1997 NBA Finals. Michael Jordan of the Bulls was the league's best player. On the day of Game 5, he was sick with the flu.

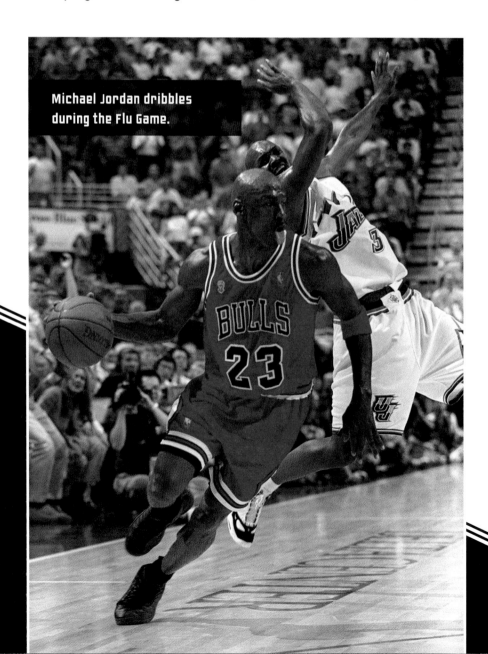

Michael Jordan dribbles during the Flu Game.

Scottie Pippen supports a sick Jordan.

But Jordan refused to sit out. In the final minute, the game was tied. Jordan took a pass from teammate Scottie Pippen. He rose up and shot a three-pointer. The ball sailed through the net to give Chicago the victory. Jordan scored 38 points in the game. Afterward, he was so tired that Pippen helped him off the court. What became known as the Flu Game remains one of the most memorable moments in NBA history.

An Epic Battle

The 2009 WNBA Finals started with a bang. In Game 1, the Indiana Fever and Phoenix Mercury battled in one of the greatest offensive explosions the league has ever seen.

With seven seconds left in the fourth quarter, the Mercury led 105–102. Indiana's Katie Douglas drilled a three-pointer to tie the game. Phoenix had a chance to win it. But Cappie Pondexter missed a tip-in. The game went to overtime.

Cappie Pondexter (*center*)

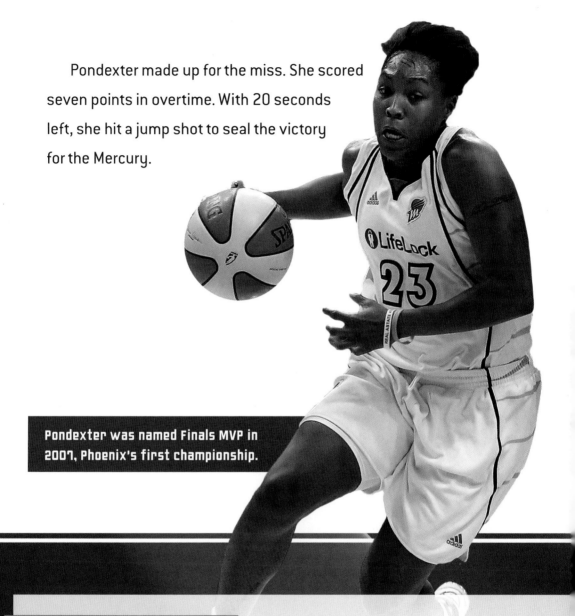

Pondexter made up for the miss. She scored seven points in overtime. With 20 seconds left, she hit a jump shot to seal the victory for the Mercury.

Pondexter was named Finals MVP in 2007, Phoenix's first championship.

Inside the Game

In 1976, the Boston Celtics and Phoenix Suns played the longest game in NBA Finals history. It went to triple overtime! Forward Glenn McDonald hit the winning shot to give Boston a 128–126 victory.

Sylvia Fowles of the Lynx looks to shoot in 2019.

CHAPTER 3

CLUTCH PERFORMERS

BASKETBALL IS A TEAM SPORT. BUT OFTEN ONE PLAYER carries a team to victory. When the game is on the line, every team wants the ball in the hands of its best player. Whether it's Michael Jordan, Cynthia Cooper, LeBron James, or Sylvia Fowles, superstars lead teams to glory.

BILL RUSSELL

No one can match the NBA Finals record of Boston's Bill Russell. In his 13-year career, he led the Celtics to 11 NBA titles. Russell did it all. He could score, defend, and rebound the ball. He even served as Boston's head coach in his final three playing seasons.

Cynthia Cooper

Sweet-shooting guard Cynthia Cooper was the first WNBA superstar. From 1997 to 2000, Cooper and the Houston Comets dominated the league. Cooper won the WNBA Finals MVP award in the league's first four seasons. The Comets won all four championships.

Michael Jordan

Michael Jordan's scoring ability, tough defense, and clutch play changed the NBA. It also made him one of the most popular athletes of all time. Jordan led the Bulls to three NBA titles in a row from 1991 to 1993. After taking two years away from basketball, Jordan returned to win three more titles from 1996 to 1998.

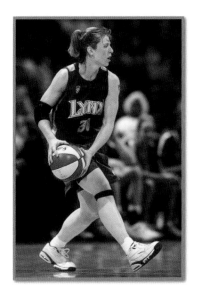

KATIE SMITH

Katie Smith was a scoring machine. She started her career with the Minnesota Lynx. But she really took off after a 2005 trade to the Detroit Shock. Smith's pinpoint three-point shooting helped the Shock win WNBA titles in 2006 and 2008. She also won three Olympic gold medals.

LEBRON JAMES

From 2011 to 2018, LeBron James never missed the NBA Finals. King James led the Miami Heat and Cleveland Cavaliers to the NBA's biggest series in eight straight seasons. James won three titles. The most memorable came in 2016. James and the Cavaliers trailed the warriors by two games in the Finals. But they came back to win Cleveland's first NBA championship.

Sylvia Fowles

Few players in basketball history have been more clutch than center Sylvia Fowles. Fowles uses her 6-foot-5 (2 m) body to bump and bang her way to the basket. She helped the Lynx win WNBA titles in 2015 and 2017. She won WNBA Finals MVP both times.

Kawhi Leonard

Kawhi Leonard is just as good at defending his basket as he is at scoring. In 2014, Leonard was the Finals MVP as the San Antonio Spurs beat the Heat. He was back in the Finals in 2019 with the Raptors. He won his second title and second Finals MVP award as Toronto took the championship.

BREANNA STEWART

Breanna Stewart of the Seattle Storm is one of the WNBA's greatest scorers. She made her first Finals appearance in 2018. Stewart was unstoppable. She averaged 25.7 points per game as the Storm swept the Washington Mystics. Her great play earned her Finals MVP honors.

Toronto Raptors fans cheer during the 2019 Finals.

CHAPTER 4
Finals Culture

THE FINALS ARE PRO BASKETBALL'S BIGGEST STAGE. Fans pack arenas to watch the action. TV cameras and reporters swarm players and coaches. The games air in more than 200 countries and 50 languages.

The women's Finals get bigger every year. Fans gather at restaurants for viewing parties. They break down the action on Facebook and Twitter. In 2017, nearly one million viewers tuned in to watch the winner-take-all Game 5 between the Sparks and Lynx.

When the final seconds tick away and only one team remains, the party begins. The WNBA winner receives the WNBA Championship Trophy. The NBA champion gets the Larry O'Brien NBA Championship Trophy.

Next comes the Finals MVP trophy, awarded to the most outstanding player in the Finals. Michael Jordan has won the trophy a record six times. Cynthia Cooper holds the WNBA record with four MVPs.

The Bill Russell NBA Finals
Most Valuable Player trophy

Fans often take to the streets to celebrate right after a championship. A few days later, they line the streets for a victory parade. It's one last party for the winners and their fans before the team begins to prepare for the next season. Then teams fight for another chance to reach the center of the basketball world— the Finals.

The Seattle Storm celebrate their third WNBA title in 2018.

Inside the Game

At 6 feet 8 inches (2 m), center Brittney Griner is the tallest WNBA player to win a championship. Griner and the Mercury won the title in 2014. But Griner isn't the tallest player in league history. That honor goes to Malgorzata Dydek at 7 feet 2 inches (2.2 m) tall.

The Raptors and their fans celebrate after the 2019 Finals.

THE CHAMPIONS

NBA Finals

Year	Champion		Year	Champion
2019	Toronto Raptors		1991	Chicago Bulls
2018	Golden State Warriors		1990	Detroit Pistons
2017	Golden State Warriors		1989	Detroit Pistons
2016	Cleveland Cavaliers		1988	Los Angeles Lakers
2015	Golden State Warriors		1987	Los Angeles Lakers
2014	San Antonio Spurs		1986	Boston Celtics
2013	Miami Heat		1985	Los Angeles Lakers
2012	Miami Heat		1984	Boston Celtics
2011	Dallas Mavericks		1983	Philadelphia 76ers
2010	Los Angeles Lakers		1982	Los Angeles Lakers
2009	Los Angeles Lakers		1981	Boston Celtics
2008	Boston Celtics		1980	Los Angeles Lakers
2007	San Antonio Spurs		1979	Seattle SuperSonics
2006	Miami Heat		1978	Washington Bullets
2005	San Antonio Spurs		1977	Portland Trail Blazers
2004	Detroit Pistons		1976	Boston Celtics
2003	San Antonio Spurs		1975	Golden State Warriors
2002	Los Angeles Lakers		1974	Boston Celtics
2001	Los Angeles Lakers		1973	New York Knicks
2000	Los Angeles Lakers		1972	Los Angeles Lakers
1999	San Antonio Spurs		1971	Milwaukee Bucks
1998	Chicago Bulls		1970	New York Knicks
1997	Chicago Bulls		1969	Boston Celtics
1996	Chicago Bulls		1968	Boston Celtics
1995	Houston Rockets		1967	Philadelphia 76ers
1994	Houston Rockets		1966	Boston Celtics
1993	Chicago Bulls		1965	Boston Celtics
1992	Chicago Bulls		1964	Boston Celtics

NBA Finals (continued)

Year	Champion	Year	Champion
1963	Boston Celtics	1953	Minneapolis Lakers
1962	Boston Celtics	1952	Minneapolis Lakers
1961	Boston Celtics	1951	Rochester Royals
1960	Boston Celtics	1950	Minneapolis Lakers
1959	Boston Celtics	1949	Minneapolis Lakers
1958	St. Louis Hawks	1948	Baltimore Bullets
1957	Boston Celtics	1947	Philadelphia Warriors
1956	Philadelphia Warriors		
1955	Syracuse Nationals		
1954	Minneapolis Lakers		

WNBA Finals

Year	Champion	Year	Champion
2019	Washington Mystics	2007	Phoenix Mercury
2018	Seattle Storm	2006	Detroit Shock
2017	Minnesota Lynx	2005	Sacramento Monarchs
2016	Los Angeles Sparks	2004	Seattle Storm
2015	Minnesota Lynx	2003	Detroit Shock
2014	Phoenix Mercury	2002	Los Angeles Sparks
2013	Minnesota Lynx	2001	Los Angeles Sparks
2012	Indiana Fever	2000	Houston Comets
2011	Minnesota Lynx	1999	Houston Comets
2010	Seattle Storm	1998	Houston Comets
2009	Phoenix Mercury	1997	Houston Comets
2008	Detroit Shock		

Glossary

center: a player who usually stays close to the basket and the middle of the court

clutch: having the ability to perform in high-pressure situations

dynasty: a team that enjoys long-term success with multiple championships

forward: a player who usually plays offense and tries to make shots

guard: a player who usually defends the team's basket

jump shot: a shot in which a player jumps with both feet to release the ball at the top of the jump

overtime: an extra five-minute period played when teams are tied at the end of regulation time

rebound: to take control of the ball after a missed shot

Further Information

Levit, Joe. *Basketball's G.O.A.T.: Michael Jordan, LeBron James, and More.* Minneapolis: Lerner Publications, 2020.

Morey, Allan. *The NBA Finals*. Minneapolis: Bellwether Media, 2019.

NBA
http://nba.com

Scheff, Matt. *Maya Moore*. Lake Elmo, MN: Focus Readers, 2019.

Sports Illustrated Kids
https://www.sikids.com/

WNBA
https://www.wnba.com/

Index

Photo Acknowledgments

Image credits: Lachlan Cunningham/Stringer/Getty Images, p. 4; Pongnathee Kluaythong/EyeEm/Getty Images, p. 5; Bettmann/Getty Images, pp. 6, 10, 19; Steve Schaeffer/AFP/Getty Images, p. 7; Ronald Martinez/Allsport/Getty Images, pp. 8, 20 (top), 21 (lower); Andy King/Getty Images, p. 9; New York Daily News Archive/Getty Images, p. 11; Andy Lyons/Getty Images, pp. 12, 13; Jeff Haynes/AFP/Getty Images, pp. 14, 15, 20 (lower); Christian Petersen/Getty Images, pp. 16, 17; Sam Wasson/Getty Images, p. 18; Mitchell Layton/Getty Images, p. 21 (top); Jevone Moore/Icon Sportswire/Getty Images, p. 22 (top); Ezra Shaw/Getty Images, p. 22 (lower); M. Anthony Nesmith/Icon Sportswire/Getty Images, p. 23; Steve Russell/Toronto Star/Getty Images, pp. 24, 27; Jason Miller/Getty Images, p. 25; Rob Carr/Getty Images, p. 26. Design elements: tamjai9/Getty Images; zhengshun tang/Getty Images; Tuomas Lehtinen/Getty Images. Cover and title page: Thearon W. Henderson/Stringer/Getty Images (right); Scott Taetsch/Getty Images (left).